ADULT CONFESSION

Conversion in Process

Carol Cowgill

Wm. C. Brown Company Publishers
Religious Education Division
Dubuque, Iowa

Nihil Obstat:
   Rev. Arthur A. Holquin

Imprimatur:
   + William R. Johnson, D.D.
   Diocese of Orange

April 10, 1984

The Nihil Obstat and Imprimatur are official declarations
that a book or pamphlet is free to doctrinal or moral
error. No implication is contained therein that those who
have granted the Nihil Obstat and Imprimatur agree with
the contents, opinions, or statements expressed.

ISBN 0-697-02030-4

Printed in the United States of America
10 9 8 7 6 5 4 3 2

Contents

iii

DEDICATION

*To all the confessors
who over the years have
taught me the meaning
of the sacrament.*

Introduction

Jesus' first and last public acts—his baptism and crucifixion—were confessions of sin. He bore and confessed the sinfulness of us all. To face this mystery with love and to allow ourselves to understand it and be judged by it are supremely difficult for Catholics. We would rather think of ourselves as slightly criminal than to face the mystery of Jesus voluntarily crucified because he understood the real quality of our sinfulness.

Theologians of the last twenty-five years have not helped us significantly. They have either maintained a deep silence or have reduced sin to a psychologized ethic that substantially denies the ability to sin to all but the self-actualized. This has left pastors and catechists to work in a vacuum, trying to reinvent the wheel.

2
Adult Confession

The time is ripe. Adults are beginning to feel the loss:

"I don't go to confession as often as I used to, because it seems so trivial."

"I feel guilty. It's been five years since I went, but I don't have anything to confess."

"I want to grow spiritually but I don't have anyone to help me."

Amid a great deal of frustration, guilt, fear and desire for God, adult Catholics are looking for a way to deepen sacramentally their commitment to following Christ.

The aim of this book is to go back to what the sacrament has been about for over a thousand years, an ongoing renewal of baptismal conversion.

The book began as a series of pamphlets for use by priests hearing confession and by catechists of adults. The present form is the result of two years' piloting, evaluation and consolidation of the material into a compact form for use by adults tired of making confession like eight-year-olds and ready to try to sacramentalize their adult experience of sin, conversion, and the mercy of God in their lives.

The underlying premise of the book is that the sacrament of Penance must be part of a process of spiritual growth marked by the desire to change and the willingness to assume responsibility for change in oneself.

SIN AND GUILT deals with the nature of sin and helps penitents to get in touch with their adult experience of guilt.

CONVERSION deals with the heart of the sacrament, helping adults move away from laundry lists that have little to do with their return to God.

FORGIVING AND BEING FORGIVEN deals with the adult meaning of forgiveness and reconciliation as contrasted with confessing simply to get things off one's chest.

IN THE CONFESSIONAL deals with the new rite for those who are uncertain about what is expected of them.

HOW OFTEN SHOULD I GO TO CONFESSION is for adults who go to confession routinely, without thinking of conversion, or who are very lax about going.

I DON'T FEEL GUILTY is for adults who go to confession basically unrepentant.

GETTING TO THE POINT is a process for examining one's action and motives so as to give a coherent accounting.

A MODEL FOR CHANGING completes the previous segment by getting adults to take responsibility for changing their behavior and attitudes.

EXAMINING YOUR CONSCIENCE is a process for daily, weekly and monthly review of life.

Included are some forms to help penitents use a journal method of preparing responsibly to celebrate their conversion and reconciliation.

Sin and Guilt

In order to understand the sacrament of Penance we need to understand sin. The difficulty in understanding sin comes from our thinking of it as something we do toward someone "out there," who is trying to push us around. Many Catholics seem to think of sin as rebelling against the arbitrary laws of a God or a Church who want to keep us under control. Many adults are unable to feel very guilty about what they perhaps perceive as legitimate civil disobedience in the city of God. For growth in understanding we need to try to get another perspective on sin and guilt.

What Do Human Beings Want?

In life we make choices because of what we want to make us happy. If we can get to the heart of what we most deeply desire, we will also come to the heart of spiritual life and death. The one thing that people everywhere long for, above all, is to be loved and desired by the person whom they love and desire. We need and want to love and be loved. If we are prevented from either loving or being loved we suffer and feel diminished. Our failure to love is the source of the human experience of guilt.

Since this desire to love is at the heart of what it means to be human, it helps us deepen our understanding of how we are made in God's image. God is a lover. We do not have to read far into the Old or New Testaments before we come face to face with his passionate desire to be understood and loved by his people. "You shall love Yahweh your God with your whole heart . . ." is not the first commandment by accident. Then Jesus expands our vision to include every person. We are to love our neighbor as ourself, to desire and reach for communion with him or her, just as God does.

Sin and Guilt

At its core sin is the refusal to approach the other person in love, whether that other is my spouse, God, myself or an "undesirable" group. Since no one can develop humanly unless he/she is loved, if I refuse to give an appropriate shape to the love needed by people and desired by God, I sin. Because in this refusal I fail to do the only thing that will bring me ultimate joy, I also experience the loss of life in the pain of guilt.

Beyond my conscious decisions, I experience guilt in the very structure of society's refusal of love, a refusal in which I often share. For example, I may never have consciously chosen to put the acquisition of property above people and their survival, but, encouraged by this culture, I often really live this way, wasting resources and perhaps living in luxury. As Christ's Spirit impels me toward love, I begin to sense the emptiness of my life. As I grow in awareness of God's love, dimension after dimension is added to guilt.

We should thank God for guilt, which, like a toothache, prevents us from ignoring the rot within, whether it takes the form of I won't love or I don't love or I can't love. Guilt sends us searching for how to become lovers.

Sins

But if sin is refusal to give love, what are those things we have thought of as sin all along—the acts of hostility, infidelity, injustice, indifference, materialism and blindness—all the offenses against the commandments and Spirit of Christ. As we mature, we begin to understand, with Jesus, that the reason such things are forbidden is precisely that they are unloving and unresponsive to persons. To go to confession fruitfully means to look at the unloving things we do, to judge ourselves guilty and to set out on the journey into loving.

Sin is real. The sacrament of Penance is for those who know sin is real, but who want to become lovers, givers of love to themselves, other people and God.

Conversion

Conversion is basically a process of falling in love with God—or of falling back in love, or more deeply in love. Conversion happens out of our experiences of guilt and sin and of longing for God. As our sin progressively cuts us off from the meaning of life as loving and turns us in on ourselves, we begin to starve and consume ourselves spiritually.

God's mercy pursues us, so that we can break out of this self-destructive spiral and begin to take the steps toward life and meaning—toward loving and knowing ourselves as loved and desired by God. For some, surrender to God the lover does not come easily. It is just as difficult—or more difficult—than the progressive surrender in love

9

to one's spouse, to mention a common experience. People experience the difficulty in different ways. Some feel pursued by the Hound of Heaven; some shrink from what seems to be a loss of humanity (Augustine); some come to the Church from intellectual conviction, shrinking from the limits of the Church's humanity (Newman); some show slow growth in understanding and commitment (Peter). For others, surrender is easier: some are instantaneously transformed (Paul); some come because they are honest, loving, searching for beauty or service. What they all experience is a profound upsurge of desire to surrender themselves more fully, within the fullness of God's love.

Let Yourself Be Called

God continually calls each one of us. In our sinfulness we can refuse to listen, or half-listen and then forget it. So it is a big help to begin to pray for the grace to hear him when he calls. We are like the boy Samuel, who was too inexperienced to understand when God called him. We need to listen more effectively.

We need to begin to recognize the sound of God's voice. When at Mass the scripture readings or homily pain us—whether because we feel inadequate, or angry with God, or despairing over the harm we have done, or irritated that yet another demand is being made—this pain is God's way of getting our attention. Another way is by attraction—we begin to wish we could be as spontaneously loving as Peter, as nobel as Isaiah, as repentant as Mary Magdalen, as full of faith as Mary, as zealous as Paul. We begin to feel the possibilities: "If only . . . " "How can I . . . " "What if . . . " We are attracted. If we attempt to respond to the God who attracts us and makes demands, conversion begins.

It is a big help to have a friend who is willing to walk with us as we begin to turn ourselves around, to give us the opportunity to talk about what we are beginning to hear, to sort through it as to whether it is growthful and open to love, and to support us in our decision to turn back to the God who is calling to us in love. It is a major function of Penance to sacramentalize the community dimension of enablement of conversion.

The major breakthrough in both conversion and Penance, the sacrament which celebrates the ongoing of conversion, is to begin to see that God's calling to us is always an act of mercy. This means that God looks at the misery we cause ourselves because of our sins and calls us out of it. In old China parents bound girls' feet as a beauty treatment. That such deformed feet caused crippling later was not considered important. The call to conversion is God's way of preventing crippling, of getting the wrappings off as quickly as possible, before we are spiritually disabled.

Some people do not understand this. They approach Penance with resentment against a God whose law, they think, makes them feel guilty. They are busy binding themselves up, and since not-growing does not seem particularly painful they resent attempts to interfere with what they want to do. By repressing their guilt they lead painless, uncomplicated lives, and like the pharisees of the gospel, feel no need to change.

Penance is for the person who knows his darkness, experiences his shame, is horrified by the harm he does: "Blessed are they who mourn."

Conversion is a lifetime process. We never succeed in freeing ourselves totally. There are times every day, every week, every year that we cry out to God for the freedom to love. Therefore, conversion is a way of life. In the celebration of Penance we join our conversion in all its moments to surrender to the torrent of the love of Christ in the Church. In this, our conversion is inserted into the heart of the crucified Lord. It becomes a sacrament, full of the promise of our transformation in love.

Forgiving and Being Forgiven

What is the thing we call forgiveness? Sometimes as children we hoped that forgiveness was a not-guilty verdict—a motherly hug telling us that what we did was not really bad at all. As adults we sometimes hope that our childish dream might prove real. But, of course, it does not.

As we reflect on times we have forgiven someone who caused us harm, we begin to perceive another logic. We know he has harmed us and we are faced with a decision: will I return the harm by excluding him from my love and concern, or not? Perhaps my parents were too strict, and I have a poor self-concept. Or my wife is using me to support her selfish life. Or my friend has used my trust in him to beat me out of a job. Or my

pastors are indifferent to my spiritual growth and I
feel spiritually retarded. These are relationships in
which I have a right to expect love, concern,
support, because we are called to share one heart
and mind in Christ.

Now, will I return the harm, or not? To forgive,
I must take the first step of fidelity toward the one
who has been unfaithful to me—because Christ is
always faithful. But this is only the first step. To
say "I forgive you, but never darken my door
again," is not really forgiveness. It is love of
enemies. Forgiveness goes a step further. When
the person who has harmed me turns back to me
and asks me to forgive, I am no longer being asked
to love an enemy but to reconstitute a friendship,
however long or painful the process might be.
Forgiveness includes a commitment to
reconciliation. Love your enemies . . . be
reconciled with your brother (mother, father,
friend, spouse, pastor).

This can be true when the person who asks for
forgiveness is ready to change his heart. If an
enemy asks forgiveness while continuing to abuse

us, we can love him, but we cannot forgive. In such a case, to forgive would be apparently to condone the evil he continues to do. Our real responsibility is to help that enemy to begin to love, and various strategies may be effective in this. We should take God as our model. Until we try to begin to love, God cannot forgive us. But he does continue to love us. His love can wear down our resistance, can arouse mature love in us. Sometimes refusal to forgive enemies is the only responsible stance, the only really loving stance.

God Invites Reconciliation

When we turn to him God tells us that not only has he forgiven our sins but he is committed to reconciliation. The sacrament of Penance is the ultimate in heart transplants. Christ gives us his heart so that we can be united as he is with God and the Church. We are reconciled as well as forgiven. This is the great surprise of being a christian. Since by our repentance we do not want to be at odds with him any longer, God no longer considers us an enemy. Forgiveness is a profound act of trust by both God and the Church that our change of heart is a real transformation, a new upsurge of life for all of us as we travel together.

For such forgiveness to happen we must know ourselves as sinners and we must be converted. Routine visits to the confessional to get things off our chest produce neither forgiveness nor reconciliation. Just by being celebrated, the sacraments give grace—here forgiveness, reconciliation, healing—if we put no obstacles in the way. The major obstacle to the sacrament of Penance's being growthful is our refusal to struggle against evil in our heart and actions; it is the refusal to enter into the process of conversion. Thinking that confessing somehow does the trick is a holdover from childhood. If you told the truth, you usually got a reprieve. This misunderstanding has grown through many years of confessing instead of many years of repenting and struggling toward the fullness of life.

The child in us cries out to God: "Love me in my sin, but don't ask me to change!" The adult in us cries out: "Love me and enable me to forgive myself and to love."

Forgiveness is possible. Reconciliation with God is real. It is even possible in the community. The proof that we are forgiven is demonstrated in our forgiving of one another. Therefore, if you are afraid that God has not forgiven you, begin the process with others. And pray: "Forgive us our trespasses as we forgive those who trespass against us."

In the Confessional

As we all know, there are a variety of ways to celebrate the sacrament of Penance today. We will not discuss the variety of options; rather, we will concentrate on the meaning of the stages of the rite.

Preparation

Your part in the preparation for confession is to discover what you have done against your vocation to love, and to turn back to the God who is calling you. The priest's part in the preparation is to pray for you.

Welcome

Jesus always welcomed sinners. Therefore, the first thing that happens is that the priest welcomes you. It would be courteous to return the greeting briefly.

Beginning

After the welcome, you begin by making the sign of the cross: "In the name of the Father and of the Son and of the Holy Spirit." The priest will join you and will then add a short prayer that God will help you make a good confession. You respond, "Amen."

Listening to God's Word

If the circumstances permit, the priest may read or ask you to read a short text from the Bible. You should listen to this reading in the context of what you plan to confess, remembering that God loves you even in your sin and calls you to turn back to him with your whole heart.

Priests sometimes skip this part of the rite. If you know that your priest will probably skip the reading, you should read one of the texts yourself before entering the confessional. A list of the main biblical passages will be found at the end of this book.

Confessing Your Sins

Since your confession has been well-prepared and well-focused, tell the priest in a simple and orderly way, what you have done, why you did it, and what graces you need. (A process for discovering this will be found in the chapter PREPARING FOR CONFESSION.) The priest may ask for clarification, which you should give briefly.

Receiving Your Penance

Many priests will talk to you about the implications of your confession and ask you what you think would be an appropriate action to take in order to make up for what you have done. At this point you might mention you plan to change. The priest will then include it in the official penance, change it if he thinks it is too much, or give you an alternative plan of action. The penance given by the priest comes in Christ's name, so it should take precedence over your original plan. Be sure to verbalize your acceptance of the penance.

Verbalizing Your Contrition

Now the priest will invite you to make an act of contrition. This prayer should express not only your regret, but your conversion, your real commitment to change. This may be in the form of an act of contrition you learned, one based on the words of scripture as found in the Rite of Penance, or a spontaneous prayer of your own. (A few such prayers will be found in Appendix 2.)

Absolution and Reconciliation

The priest will now extend his hands over your head, saying, "God the Father of mercy, through the death and resurrection of his Son, has reconciled the world to himself and sent the Holy Spirit among us for the forgiveness of sins; through the ministry of the Church may God give you pardon and peace, and I absolve you from your sins in the name of the Father and of the Son and of the Holy Spirit." He then makes the sign of the cross over you. These words and actions indicate that your forgiveness and reconciliation come from the Father's mercy, that they are united to Christ's death and resurrection and that the Spirit and the Church are the agents of conversion, forgiveness and reconciliation.

Praising God

The priest then invites you to thank God for his mercy saying, "Give thanks to the Lord for he is good." Your response is "His mercy endures forever."

Dismissal

The priest then invites you to go in peace. Your response is "Amen," after which you leave.

How Often Should I Go to Confession

Penance is the sacrament of post-baptismal conversion. And conversion is a return to or a deepening of being in love with God. The how-often can be answered only with reference to how conversion is going on in your life. There are big conversions, major turning to love, and there are small ones.

Loving is not easy. When we have violated others' rights to our love—the rights of our children, our spouse, our fellow citizens, our parish, our God—and we want to turn to loving, we still have the problem of overcoming the breach. For example, if you were unfaithful to your spouse and now regret it, how can you go back to walk with the one who had to walk alone?

Where will you meet him/her on the way? Some people pick up the pieces and act as if nothing had happened. But this is unrealistic. There is no way to undo its having happened. But what *you* cannot do, the other can. By forgiveness, he/she can change course to rejoin you. When we go to each other with, "I am sorry, will you please forgive?", the loving forgiveness of those we have hurt enables us to know that our attempts to love are acceptable. We can be assured that the one we have hurt is once again willing to entrust himself or herself to our good will now and in the future.

To be so valued and trusted is tremendously freeing. Forgiveness frees us to love. This is the freedom to which Christ calls us in this sacrament. People sometimes wonder why we should confess our sins to other sinful human beings. One reason is that as our sin has social repercussions, so does our confession and repentance. Moreover, we humans need to experience simple human forgiveness in order to come to believe in God's forgiveness and in order, finally, to forgive ourselves. In the confessional the priest sacramentalizes the presence of the Father, of

Christ in his Church, and of the whole human race whom our sin has damaged. He offers both forgiveness and reconciliation.

How Often Should I Go to Confession?

The sacrament of Penance means that I know that, baptized into a community as I am, I am not alone in my struggle. Since my sin has affected the Church, my conversion is also the profound concern of the Church, which stands with me and struggles with me toward love.

The Church celebrates the conversion of its catechumens and penitents primarily during Lent. Therefore, we should all join the others at least then. Other than that it depends on how seriously you are making your spiritual journey. If you strive for a totally loving life, then conversion is the name of the game, and you will celebrate Penance within the rhythm of your progressing. Many Catholics seem to follow the liturgical year—Lent,

Easter, Pentecost, Advent. These are the privileged times of grace. Others with a great devotion to God's love will add a celebration of the sacrament before the feasts of the Lord and first Fridays. Others who are wrestling with a very difficult tendency to sin and who are constantly tempted, will celebrate the sacrament weekly or oftener.

People who have undergone a renewal experience in a parish renewal retreat or adult education program, will celebrate the new conversion that the experience has brought into their lives. People in a period of major transition may want to review a large portion of their lives, in order to deepen their reorientation to love.

The rule is probably like that which decides how often you go to the doctor or take medicine. You cannot be mechanical—it depends on the illness and its progress. The sacrament should represent a healing process. How often may mean twice a month, once a month, three times a year— but at least once a year, during Lent. Less than once a year is a sign of loving the darkness, as with people who avoid their annual physical because they do not want to know and have to deal with how they are.

Too often conversion is marked by routine, going into the confessional with lists of evil actions and without any real concern to change one's life around. Perhaps a rule of thumb is to ask the priest for a penance that will really help you turn your life around. When you have tried to do the penance and you are ready to describe how well the process of change is going, you can prepare to celebrate the sacrament again.

I Don't Feel Guilty

Our experience of adult guilt is a recognition that because we have not given the love we ought, we are diminished and impaired. Yet we all know people whose lives are profoundly unloving and yet who apparently do not feel guilt. For example, a man may make a confession of repeated adultery, which he does not perceive as unloving to his wife, only as forbidden. Some of us have great denial skills: "Who, me? I'm not a crook!"—to the astonished ears and eyes of the world.

Self-Deception

Typically such people also distance themselves from the Church. "The Church" says

30

this is wrong, but I don't think so. "The Church" says this is evil, but who is being hurt? The fantasy of victimless crime becomes their ethical criterion. "Who is being hurt?" says the woman aborting her child. No victim? "Who is being hurt?" says the father sexually abusing his daughter. "It is a natural expression of love." No victims? "Who is being hurt?" says the business man charging exorbitant interest on personal loans. No victims? "Who is being hurt when two consenting adults live together?" No victims?

Why do we deceive ourselves? Why do we deny our refusal to care for, reverence and nurture others? Of course there must be more than one answer to such questions. Perhaps I am afraid that if admitting my unlovingness even to myself, no one will be left to love me. Perhaps I am afraid that if I face my guilt, I will have to leave the security of constricted responsibilities for the freedom of growth. In both these cases the underlying problem is despair—I despair that all spiritual growth is toward love and joy. Such despair refuses to trust what God tells us about our loveableness and promise.

Guilt grows as empathy grows. Empathy grows as we identify ourselves with others in pain—through actual contact or through literature, drama movies, radio, TV. Eventually we come to see ourselves not only in those who are suffering pain, but also in those inflicting pain— and we try to put an end to it.

The person who cannot admit his/her guilt cannot celebrate the sacrament of Penance: "I came to call not the righteous but sinners." Such a person has not made the first step.

Penance Is for
the Guilty

The sacrament of Penance can be celebrated only by guilty people. It is a sacrament of the struggle of guilt over sin.

What about people who are ambivalent? They do not admit guilt, yet they go to confession because they hope getting it off their chests will pay off an unreasonable God or Church. Such people need a breakthrough. One way is to give up denying their guilt, and simply to ask the community, "Am I guilty?"; to ask God, "Am I guilty?" "Judge me, O Lord, and know my heart." They need to let God speak through the community, especially since they often cannot directly ask the people whom they harm. They must ask the victims of others' injustice, child abuse, infidelity, lack of concern, and listen to their bitterness and to God's "The more I spoke the more you turned your backs . . . you despise my words . . . you shall be called Not-my-people."

"I don't feel guilty." "Am I my brother's keeper?" "What is wrong with what I have done?" are Cain's responses.

So, if you do not think you are guilty of anything, talk with the believing community, with your priest and the catechists; begin to read the gospel, the prophets; talk the situation over with Christ crucified. When your faith tells you: "Yes, I am unloving . . . I want to love"—even if your emotions are not very involved—you are ready for confession. Until then it is better not to go. Rather, pray to know the truth about yourself.

Getting to
the Point

When we were children we were taught to mention the circumstances surrounding our mortal sins. What our teachers forgot to tell us is what the pertinent circumstances are. The result is that priests often sit in the confessional listening to dizzying accounts of how when Harry and Colleen were in town from Peoria over the weekend and the family was going to Newport Beach for dinner, the eleven and twelve-year-olds went wandering off with the dog, so that her husband was angry, and she got so frustrated that she told her husband to go to hell.

Circumstantial detail should be limited to what effects the nature of the sin, its significance in your spiritual life and perhaps its consequences

34

in the lives of the persons harmed. What would such a confession be like in actual practice? The answer to this question depends on how you have thought through your sinfulness. It would be a good idea to be able to answer the following questions before entering the confessional. Please refer to the following Checklist as you read.

What Is the General Direction God Is Calling You in Your Spiritual Life?

For example, if you are resisting a call to a more apostolic life, your spiritual growth will be affected by refusal to move out toward others, even if your moral stance and action otherwise seem perfect. (See Checklist, #1.)

How Are You Diminishing Yourself and Others?

Concretely, what have you done—whether by belittling, misjudging, abusing, being indifferent to, ignoring, cheating, despising others? Be concrete: Who was involved? How did you do

1. AS I NOW SEE IT, GOD IS CALLING ME TO BE MORE LOVING AND RESPONSIVE

BY _____

_____

2. WHOSE RIGHT TO TRUST AND LOVE DID I VIOLATE?

_____

INDIVIDUAL/GROUP

3. WHAT DID THIS PERSON HAVE A RIGHT TO EXPECT FROM ME AS A LOVER?

_____

4. HOW HAVE I FAILED TO LOVE ENOUGH SINCE MY LAST CONFESSION? (BE SPE-

CIFIC) _____

_____

_____

_____

_____

5. IS THIS PART OF A LONGER STRUGGLE? HOW FAR BACK?_____

_____

6. WHY DO I REFUSE TO GIVE THIS LOVE?

_____

7. THE GRACES I NEED TO HANDLE NO. 3, 4, 6 ABOVE ARE

    3. _____

    4. _____

    6. _____

8. HOW HAVE I RESPONDED TO THESE GRACES GIVEN IN THE PAST? _____

_____

9. I HAVE ASKED GOD'S FORGIVENESS AND THE FORGIVENESS OF THOSE I HAVE

HURT. I ASK THE CHURCH TO PRAY FOR ME. _____

10. I WILL DO THE FOLLOWING TO INTENSIFY MY STRUGGLE TO LOVE

_____

_____

them harm? Be sure you include both yourself and Christ in the list of those harmed. How often you did it is a clue to its depth. (See Checklist, #3–5.)

Why Did You Do This?

Because I think I am better than he is; I have no self-control; I want power over him; I am full of self pity; I am afraid to trust Christ; I don't want to have God be above me? There are many other possibilities, so you must find what fits you. (See Checklist, #6.)

As You Reflect on the Above, What Graces Do You Discover You Need?

Humility, patience, desire to serve, a sense of humor, faith, chastity—what? Ask God for these graces. (See Checklist, #7–8.)

Until you make a plan for changing (see the next chapter) you are not quite ready for confession. It would be important to talk the matter over with your spiritual guide, catechist or a good friend who cares about your spiritual growth, until you can put your spiritual accounting into some significant order.

When you do all this, your confession would be clearly focused. In the example with which we started, the confession would go like this: "I insulted my husband in public because I was frustrated over my children's irresponsibility. The reason why I was frustrated is that I wanted to impress some relations with how well I maintained control in the family. I have been too ashamed to ask my husband's forgiveness yet." This is something the priest will be able to deal with.

A Model for Changing

Sin, Guilt, and Conversion

Once we allow our guilt to convict us of being unloving persons, we are ready to begin the process of living by God's Spirit (conversion). The sacrament of Penance is the Church's celebration of this transformation in our lives. Since we have celebrated the sacrament many times and yet remain unloving in our attitude and behavior, we discover that we need some sort of plan for bringing about real changes in ourselves.

In order to change, we need a strong conviction that our sinfulness is not terminal. We do experience spiritual death or near-death and

39

we experience how we spread it to others. However, Christ has already given us his Spirit, the very life of God welling up from our greatest depth. Therefore, sin need never be terminal. This is Christ's promise and the universal experience of a Church that has struggled with sin for 2000 years. Relying, therefore, on the Spirit's driving us toward God's life of love, we can begin to initiate change.

The following will use the Checklist as a point of reference.

Preliminaries

There are four preliminaries to change:

1. to identify our unloving behavior (Checklist #3, 4);
2. to identify the unloving attitude that underlies this behavior (Checklist #6);
3. to identify the grace that we need (Checklist #7, 8);
4. to ask for forgiveness and the grace we need to change (Checklist #9).

1. AS I NOW SEE IT, GOD IS CALLING ME TO BE MORE LOVING AND RESPONSIVE

BY _____

_____

2. WHOSE RIGHT TO TRUST AND LOVE DID I VIOLATE?

_____

INDIVIDUAL/GROUP

3. WHAT DID THIS PERSON HAVE A RIGHT TO EXPECT FROM ME AS A LOVER?

_____

4. HOW HAVE I FAILED TO LOVE ENOUGH SINCE MY LAST CONFESSION? (BE SPE-

CIFIC) _____

_____

_____

_____

_____

5. IS THIS PART OF A LONGER STRUGGLE? HOW FAR BACK?_____

_____

6. WHY DO I REFUSE TO GIVE THIS LOVE?

_____

7. THE GRACES I NEED TO HANDLE NO. 3, 4, 6 ABOVE ARE

    3. _____

    4. _____

    6. _____

8. HOW HAVE I RESPONDED TO THESE GRACES GIVEN IN THE PAST? _____

_____

9. I HAVE ASKED GOD'S FORGIVENESS AND THE FORGIVENESS OF THOSE I HAVE

HURT. I ASK THE CHURCH TO PRAY FOR ME. _____

10. I WILL DO THE FOLLOWING TO INTENSIFY MY STRUGGLE TO LOVE

_____

_____

For example, let us say that WHAT YOU DID was to fail to give a co-worker credit. When the supervisor praised a good job, you took full credit for it. What ATTITUDE underlay this injustice? Let us say that you did this because you felt that your job was a little too shakey and you were afraid to jeopardize it by sharing credit. WHAT you did and WHY are two distinct things and need two graces: first, generous truthfulness, and second, trusting God to provide the work you need. Then you ask God's forgiveness and the graces you need.

Making a Plan

Now you are in a position to make a plan to change this BEHAVIOR of not giving credit where credit is due. First, decide WHAT you will do. In this example you decide to do two things: you will go to the supervisor and clarify your co-worker's role in the work and you will praise your co-worker once to a third party.

Now WHEN will you do this? *Decide:* I will go to the supervisor first thing in the morning and will brag about my co-worker to a third person over lunch.

The next question is HOW are you going to remind yourself to think of all this? *Decide:* for the first, when I say my usual good morning to the supervisor I will add the clarification lightly. For the second, when the third person and I are exchanging office gossip, I will slip in my remark.

Your plan is now ready, simple, clear and able to be checked up on.

Now for the second item, your anxiety about your job and lack of trust in God. Since this is an ATTITUDE and not just an action, it is less simple to find WHAT to do. Let us say that you decide that you need to read some scripture on gospel poverty, and so you plan to spend ten minutes reading Matthew, about Mary and Joseph's not finding an inn for Jesus' birth. You will do this, asking these two saints to pray for you to be more trusting. WHEN will you do this? You know that today and tomorrow will be very busy days, but that on Wednesday the family will be out. So you decide to make this meditation on Wednesday right after dinner and before you watch the news.

HOW will you remind yourself of this? You decide that the reminder will be to put a heavy red circle around the Wednesday listing for the six o'clock news in the TV guide.

By doing all of this you are changing your behavior, and you will be able to feel good about your commitment of change.

Getting Help

Although such a plan for change is not difficult, it might become mind-boggling, considering how often we do or think hurtful things. A DAILY EXAMINATION of conscience is the easiest way of keeping a clear focus. Another way would be to have a spiritual friend or helper who could talk to you about your conversion and help you to set priorities. Trying to work on ten things simultaneously scatters your energy. Working on one or two things at a time makes better sense. Your pastor may be able to recommend such a helper from the pastoral staff.

When finally you bring such a commitment to change to the sacrament of Penance you will experience what the sacrament is intended to be—the sacrament of an adult believer's taking his/her spiritual growth as a priority and working at it seriously and creatively. If you are celebrating the sacrament well, you may find that the penance given by the priest is a recommendation that you put your plan into effect.

Examining Your Conscience

The best way to focus your confession is to have a regular process of examination of conscience. The following is a simple plan for keeping in touch with your spiritual development.

Daily Examination of Conscience

The daily examination of conscience is the secret to effective confessions. If you do this every day, you will never again find yourself with a vague sense that something is seriously wrong with your relationship with God and other people. Because the daily examination covers such a short period of time, it is also easy.

Begin with a short reflection of the general direction that God is leading you, your vocation, and the graces you have received that day—at prayer, at work, when relaxing, when serving. Write these down briefly.

How did you respond to these graces positively? Write this down.

How did refusal to love God, yourself and others surface today? What was done unlovingly; how was the person hurt (include God and yourself); what attitude underlay your action? Once you realized what you had done, what did you do to undo it? If nothing, why not?

What is your concrete plan for dealing with these things tomorrow? Write it down.

Think over what you are to do tomorrow. Do you foresee any situations that might be problems? Make a plan to prevent the problem from arising.

Finish your examination, thanking God for his grace, asking for forgiveness for what was unloving and for the grace you need to change.

Once a Week

Take your daily examinations and begin to summarize and focus the issues. What are the repeated actions? Classify these into groups: e.g., cutting people down, nagging, dishonesty in accounting, indulging in sexual fantasies, etc. Is one of these more frequent or more intense than the others? Who are the people you hurt by these actions (include yourself and God)? Is there one person who is bearing the brunt of your failure to love? Why him, her, you?

Is there an action plan for next week flowing from all this? If so, make it and write it down. Having a chat with your spiritual helper might be useful at this point.

Once a Month or Before Confession

Proceed as above, except look over only the weekly reviews. Consolidate these by trying to combine items that belong together. For example, if you discover that anxiety and lack of trust in God underlie several things you do, you might want to concentrate on these and confess your sins this way: "I begin to see that I don't trust God very much. Because I let myself worry that he would not help me, I did (1) . . . (2) . . . (3) . . . "

If you discover that you are harming one person most, you might say something like: "I am making my second youngest son a scapegoat. Whenever I am angry or upset I take it out on him, because he is a disappointment to me. I want him to go to college, and he wants to be a mechanic. I have been laying into him so much that he hates to come home."

If you find one sinful activity predominating you might mention it: "This month I have a terrible time with deliberate sexual fantasies, especially while watching TV. It has me distracted from my work, especially when women are around. I think that this is probably caused by too much TV and not enough exercise, so I started bowling more, and it is better now."

Once a Year

At New Year or during Lent or your annual retreat, it might be helpful to spend a day reflecting on your monthly summaries, so as to get an overview of where God has led you so far and how you are doing. Set your course for the next year, go to confession, and burn the previous year's papers. It is time to start fresh.

This examination takes about ten minutes a day and is one of the best tools for spiritual growth and for insuring that going to confession will be a real response to grace and a celebration of growth to the fullness of life.

Forms for Preparing for Confession

How to Use
These Forms

1. Who are the individuals or groups whom you are conscious of not being right with? Place their names in the #2 line of each form (one name per form). The last two forms should deal with you yourself and with God. Use as many forms as necessary.

2. Fill out the forms which have names on them. Try to be complete. Do not skip the forms which deal with God and yourself.

3. Do any forms deal with the same issues? Indicate the forms that can be combined because they deal with the same dimension of sin.

4. Place the forms in order of priority.

5. If you go to confession infrequently (less than four times a year) cover all the forms in your confession.

6. If you go to confession regularly and frequently, make a selection of the most urgent items in the light of how God is leading you. You are now ready for confession.

1. AS I NOW SEE IT, GOD IS CALLING ME TO BE MORE LOVING AND RESPONSIVE

BY _____

_____

2. WHOSE RIGHT TO TRUST AND LOVE DID I VIOLATE?

_____

INDIVIDUAL/GROUP

3. WHAT DID THIS PERSON HAVE A RIGHT TO EXPECT FROM ME AS A LOVER?

_____

4. HOW HAVE I FAILED TO LOVE ENOUGH SINCE MY LAST CONFESSION? (BE SPE-

CIFIC) _____

_____

_____

_____

_____

5. IS THIS PART OF A LONGER STRUGGLE? HOW FAR BACK?_____

_____

6. WHY DO I REFUSE TO GIVE THIS LOVE?

_____

7. THE GRACES I NEED TO HANDLE NO. 3, 4, 6 ABOVE ARE

   3. _____

   4. _____

   6. _____

8. HOW HAVE I RESPONDED TO THESE GRACES GIVEN IN THE PAST? _____

_____

9. I HAVE ASKED GOD'S FORGIVENESS AND THE FORGIVENESS OF THOSE I HAVE

HURT. I ASK THE CHURCH TO PRAY FOR ME. _____

10. I WILL DO THE FOLLOWING TO INTENSIFY MY STRUGGLE TO LOVE

_____

_____

Appendix 1

Biblical
Meditations for
Penance

Isaiah 53:4–6

Ezekiel 11:19–20

Matthew 6:14–15

Mark 1:14–15

Luke 6:31–38

Luke 15:1–7

John 20:19–23

Romans 5:8–9

Ephesians 5:1–2

Colossians 1:12–14

Colossians 3:8–10, 12–17

1 John 1:6–7, 9

Appendix 2

Acts of Contrition

My God,
I am sorry for my sins with all my heart.
In choosing to do wrong and failing to do good,
I have sinned against you
whom I should love above all things.
I firmly intend, with your help,
to do penance,
to sin no more,
and to avoid whatever leads to sin.
Our Savior Jesus Christ
suffered and died for us.
In his name, my God, have mercy.

From *Rite of Penance* © 1974, International Committee on English in the Liturgy, Inc.

Remember, Lord, your compassion and mercy
  which you showed long ago.
Do not recall the sins and failings of my youth.
In your mercy remember me, Lord, because of
  your goodness.

Wash me from my guilt
and cleanse me of my sin.
I acknowledge my offense;
my sin is before me always.

Father, I have sinned against you
and am not worthy to be called your son.
Be merciful to me, a sinner.

Father of mercy,
like the prodigal son
I return to you and say:
"I have sinned against you
and am no longer worthy to be called your son."
Christ Jesus, Savior of the world,
I pray with the repentant thief
to whom you promised paradise:
"Lord, remember me in your kingdom."
Holy Spirit, fountain of love,
I call on you with trust:
"Purify my heart,
and help me walk as a child of light."

Lord Jesus,
you opened the eyes of the blind,
healed the sick,
forgave the sinful woman,
and after Peter's denial confirmed him in your
     love.
Listen to my prayer:
forgive all my sins,
renew your love in my heart,
help me to live in perfect unity with my fellow
     Christians
that I may proclaim your saving power to all the
     world.

Lord Jesus,
you chose to be called the friend of sinners.
By your saving death and resurrection
free me from my sins.
May your peace take root in my heart
and bring forth a harvest
of love, holiness, and truth.

58
Adult Confession

Lord Jesus Christ,
you are the Lamb of God;
you take away the sins of the world.
Through the grace of the Spirit
restore me to friendship with your Father,
cleanse me from every stain of sin
in the blood you shed for me,
and raise me to new life
for the glory of your name.

Lord God,
in your goodness have mercy on me:
do not look on my sins,
take away all my guilt.
Create in me a clean heart
and renew within me an upright spirit.

Lord Jesus, Son of God,
have mercy on me, a sinner.

Personal Notes

1. AS I NOW SEE IT, GOD IS CALLING ME TO BE MORE LOVING AND RESPONSIVE

BY _____

_____

2. WHOSE RIGHT TO TRUST AND LOVE DID I VIOLATE?

_____

INDIVIDUAL/GROUP

3. WHAT DID THIS PERSON HAVE A RIGHT TO EXPECT FROM ME AS A LOVER?

_____

4. HOW HAVE I FAILED TO LOVE ENOUGH SINCE MY LAST CONFESSION? (BE SPE-

CIFIC) _____

_____

_____

_____

_____

5. IS THIS PART OF A LONGER STRUGGLE? HOW FAR BACK?_____

_____

6. WHY DO I REFUSE TO GIVE THIS LOVE?

_____

7. THE GRACES I NEED TO HANDLE NO. 3, 4, 6 ABOVE ARE

    3. _____

    4. _____

    6. _____

8. HOW HAVE I RESPONDED TO THESE GRACES GIVEN IN THE PAST? _____

_____

9. I HAVE ASKED GOD'S FORGIVENESS AND THE FORGIVENESS OF THOSE I HAVE

HURT. I ASK THE CHURCH TO PRAY FOR ME. _____

10. I WILL DO THE FOLLOWING TO INTENSIFY MY STRUGGLE TO LOVE

_____

_____

1. AS I NOW SEE IT, GOD IS CALLING ME TO BE MORE LOVING AND RESPONSIVE

BY _____

_____

2. WHOSE RIGHT TO TRUST AND LOVE DID I VIOLATE?

_____

INDIVIDUAL/GROUP

3. WHAT DID THIS PERSON HAVE A RIGHT TO EXPECT FROM ME AS A LOVER?

_____

4. HOW HAVE I FAILED TO LOVE ENOUGH SINCE MY LAST CONFESSION? (BE SPE-

CIFIC) _____

_____

_____

_____

_____

5. IS THIS PART OF A LONGER STRUGGLE? HOW FAR BACK?_____

_____

6. WHY DO I REFUSE TO GIVE THIS LOVE?

_____

7. THE GRACES I NEED TO HANDLE NO. 3, 4, 6 ABOVE ARE

    3. _____

    4. _____

    6. _____

8. HOW HAVE I RESPONDED TO THESE GRACES GIVEN IN THE PAST? _____

_____

9. I HAVE ASKED GOD'S FORGIVENESS AND THE FORGIVENESS OF THOSE I HAVE

HURT. I ASK THE CHURCH TO PRAY FOR ME. _____

10. I WILL DO THE FOLLOWING TO INTENSIFY MY STRUGGLE TO LOVE

_____

_____

1. AS I NOW SEE IT, GOD IS CALLING ME TO BE MORE LOVING AND RESPONSIVE

BY _____

_____

2. WHOSE RIGHT TO TRUST AND LOVE DID I VIOLATE?

_____

INDIVIDUAL/GROUP

3. WHAT DID THIS PERSON HAVE A RIGHT TO EXPECT FROM ME AS A LOVER?

_____

4. HOW HAVE I FAILED TO LOVE ENOUGH SINCE MY LAST CONFESSION? (BE SPE-

CIFIC) _____

_____

_____

_____

_____

5. IS THIS PART OF A LONGER STRUGGLE? HOW FAR BACK?_____

_____

6. WHY DO I REFUSE TO GIVE THIS LOVE?

_____

7. THE GRACES I NEED TO HANDLE NO. 3, 4, 6 ABOVE ARE

   3. _____

   4. _____

   6. _____

8. HOW HAVE I RESPONDED TO THESE GRACES GIVEN IN THE PAST? _____

_____

9. I HAVE ASKED GOD'S FORGIVENESS AND THE FORGIVENESS OF THOSE I HAVE

HURT. I ASK THE CHURCH TO PRAY FOR ME. _____

10. I WILL DO THE FOLLOWING TO INTENSIFY MY STRUGGLE TO LOVE

_____

_____

1. AS I NOW SEE IT, GOD IS CALLING ME TO BE MORE LOVING AND RESPONSIVE

BY _____

_____

2. WHOSE RIGHT TO TRUST AND LOVE DID I VIOLATE?

_____

INDIVIDUAL/GROUP

3. WHAT DID THIS PERSON HAVE A RIGHT TO EXPECT FROM ME AS A LOVER?

_____

4. HOW HAVE I FAILED TO LOVE ENOUGH SINCE MY LAST CONFESSION? (BE SPE-

CIFIC) _____

_____

_____

_____

_____

5. IS THIS PART OF A LONGER STRUGGLE? HOW FAR BACK?_____

_____

6. WHY DO I REFUSE TO GIVE THIS LOVE?

_____

7. THE GRACES I NEED TO HANDLE NO. 3, 4, 6 ABOVE ARE

   3. _____

   4. _____

   6. _____

8. HOW HAVE I RESPONDED TO THESE GRACES GIVEN IN THE PAST? _____

_____

9. I HAVE ASKED GOD'S FORGIVENESS AND THE FORGIVENESS OF THOSE I HAVE

HURT. I ASK THE CHURCH TO PRAY FOR ME. _____

10. I WILL DO THE FOLLOWING TO INTENSIFY MY STRUGGLE TO LOVE

_____

_____

1. AS I NOW SEE IT, GOD IS CALLING ME TO BE MORE LOVING AND RESPONSIVE

BY _____

_____

2. WHOSE RIGHT TO TRUST AND LOVE DID I VIOLATE?

_____

INDIVIDUAL/GROUP

3. WHAT DID THIS PERSON HAVE A RIGHT TO EXPECT FROM ME AS A LOVER?

_____

4. HOW HAVE I FAILED TO LOVE ENOUGH SINCE MY LAST CONFESSION? (BE SPE-

CIFIC) _____

_____

_____

_____

_____

5. IS THIS PART OF A LONGER STRUGGLE? HOW FAR BACK?_____

_____

6. WHY DO I REFUSE TO GIVE THIS LOVE?

_____

7. THE GRACES I NEED TO HANDLE NO. 3, 4, 6 ABOVE ARE

3. _____

4. _____

6. _____

8. HOW HAVE I RESPONDED TO THESE GRACES GIVEN IN THE PAST? _____

_____

9. I HAVE ASKED GOD'S FORGIVENESS AND THE FORGIVENESS OF THOSE I HAVE

HURT. I ASK THE CHURCH TO PRAY FOR ME. _____

10. I WILL DO THE FOLLOWING TO INTENSIFY MY STRUGGLE TO LOVE

_____

_____

1. AS I NOW SEE IT, GOD IS CALLING ME TO BE MORE LOVING AND RESPONSIVE

BY _____

_____

2. WHOSE RIGHT TO TRUST AND LOVE DID I VIOLATE?

_____

INDIVIDUAL/GROUP

3. WHAT DID THIS PERSON HAVE A RIGHT TO EXPECT FROM ME AS A LOVER?

_____

4. HOW HAVE I FAILED TO LOVE ENOUGH SINCE MY LAST CONFESSION? (BE SPE-

CIFIC) _____

_____

_____

_____

_____

5. IS THIS PART OF A LONGER STRUGGLE? HOW FAR BACK?_____

_____

6. WHY DO I REFUSE TO GIVE THIS LOVE?

_____

7. THE GRACES I NEED TO HANDLE NO. 3, 4, 6 ABOVE ARE

    3. _____

    4. _____

    6. _____

8. HOW HAVE I RESPONDED TO THESE GRACES GIVEN IN THE PAST? _____

_____

9. I HAVE ASKED GOD'S FORGIVENESS AND THE FORGIVENESS OF THOSE I HAVE

HURT. I ASK THE CHURCH TO PRAY FOR ME. _____

10. I WILL DO THE FOLLOWING TO INTENSIFY MY STRUGGLE TO LOVE

_____

_____

1. AS I NOW SEE IT, GOD IS CALLING ME TO BE MORE LOVING AND RESPONSIVE

BY _____

_____

2. WHOSE RIGHT TO TRUST AND LOVE DID I VIOLATE?

_____

INDIVIDUAL/GROUP

3. WHAT DID THIS PERSON HAVE A RIGHT TO EXPECT FROM ME AS A LOVER?

_____

4. HOW HAVE I FAILED TO LOVE ENOUGH SINCE MY LAST CONFESSION? (BE SPE-

CIFIC) _____

_____

_____

_____

_____

5. IS THIS PART OF A LONGER STRUGGLE? HOW FAR BACK?_____

_____

6. WHY DO I REFUSE TO GIVE THIS LOVE?

_____

7. THE GRACES I NEED TO HANDLE NO. 3, 4, 6 ABOVE ARE

    3. _____

    4. _____

    6. _____

8. HOW HAVE I RESPONDED TO THESE GRACES GIVEN IN THE PAST? _____

_____

9. I HAVE ASKED GOD'S FORGIVENESS AND THE FORGIVENESS OF THOSE I HAVE

HURT. I ASK THE CHURCH TO PRAY FOR ME. _____

10. I WILL DO THE FOLLOWING TO INTENSIFY MY STRUGGLE TO LOVE

_____

_____

1. AS I NOW SEE IT, GOD IS CALLING ME TO BE MORE LOVING AND RESPONSIVE

BY _____

_____

2. WHOSE RIGHT TO TRUST AND LOVE DID I VIOLATE?

_____

INDIVIDUAL/GROUP

3. WHAT DID THIS PERSON HAVE A RIGHT TO EXPECT FROM ME AS A LOVER?

_____

4. HOW HAVE I FAILED TO LOVE ENOUGH SINCE MY LAST CONFESSION? (BE SPE-

CIFIC) _____

_____

_____

_____

_____

5. IS THIS PART OF A LONGER STRUGGLE? HOW FAR BACK?_____

_____

6. WHY DO I REFUSE TO GIVE THIS LOVE?

_____

7. THE GRACES I NEED TO HANDLE NO. 3, 4, 6 ABOVE ARE

    3. _____

    4. _____

    6. _____

8. HOW HAVE I RESPONDED TO THESE GRACES GIVEN IN THE PAST? _____

_____

9. I HAVE ASKED GOD'S FORGIVENESS AND THE FORGIVENESS OF THOSE I HAVE

HURT. I ASK THE CHURCH TO PRAY FOR ME. _____

10. I WILL DO THE FOLLOWING TO INTENSIFY MY STRUGGLE TO LOVE

_____

_____

1. AS I NOW SEE IT, GOD IS CALLING ME TO BE MORE LOVING AND RESPONSIVE

BY _____

_____

2. WHOSE RIGHT TO TRUST AND LOVE DID I VIOLATE?

_____

INDIVIDUAL/GROUP

3. WHAT DID THIS PERSON HAVE A RIGHT TO EXPECT FROM ME AS A LOVER?

_____

4. HOW HAVE I FAILED TO LOVE ENOUGH SINCE MY LAST CONFESSION? (BE SPE-

CIFIC) _____

_____

_____

_____

_____

5. IS THIS PART OF A LONGER STRUGGLE? HOW FAR BACK?_____

_____

6. WHY DO I REFUSE TO GIVE THIS LOVE?

_____

7. THE GRACES I NEED TO HANDLE NO. 3, 4, 6 ABOVE ARE

    3. _____

    4. _____

    6. _____

8. HOW HAVE I RESPONDED TO THESE GRACES GIVEN IN THE PAST? _____

_____

9. I HAVE ASKED GOD'S FORGIVENESS AND THE FORGIVENESS OF THOSE I HAVE

HURT. I ASK THE CHURCH TO PRAY FOR ME. _____

10. I WILL DO THE FOLLOWING TO INTENSIFY MY STRUGGLE TO LOVE

_____

_____

1. AS I NOW SEE IT, GOD IS CALLING ME TO BE MORE LOVING AND RESPONSIVE

BY _____

_____

2. WHOSE RIGHT TO TRUST AND LOVE DID I VIOLATE?

_____

INDIVIDUAL/GROUP

3. WHAT DID THIS PERSON HAVE A RIGHT TO EXPECT FROM ME AS A LOVER?

_____

4. HOW HAVE I FAILED TO LOVE ENOUGH SINCE MY LAST CONFESSION? (BE SPE-

CIFIC) _____

_____

_____

_____

_____

5. IS THIS PART OF A LONGER STRUGGLE? HOW FAR BACK?_____

_____

6. WHY DO I REFUSE TO GIVE THIS LOVE?

_____

7. THE GRACES I NEED TO HANDLE NO. 3, 4, 6 ABOVE ARE

    3. _____

    4. _____

    6. _____

8. HOW HAVE I RESPONDED TO THESE GRACES GIVEN IN THE PAST? _____

_____

9. I HAVE ASKED GOD'S FORGIVENESS AND THE FORGIVENESS OF THOSE I HAVE

HURT. I ASK THE CHURCH TO PRAY FOR ME. _____

10. I WILL DO THE FOLLOWING TO INTENSIFY MY STRUGGLE TO LOVE

_____

_____

1. AS I NOW SEE IT, GOD IS CALLING ME TO BE MORE LOVING AND RESPONSIVE

BY _____

_____

2. WHOSE RIGHT TO TRUST AND LOVE DID I VIOLATE?

_____

INDIVIDUAL/GROUP

3. WHAT DID THIS PERSON HAVE A RIGHT TO EXPECT FROM ME AS A LOVER?

_____

4. HOW HAVE I FAILED TO LOVE ENOUGH SINCE MY LAST CONFESSION? (BE SPE-

CIFIC) _____

_____

_____

_____

_____

5. IS THIS PART OF A LONGER STRUGGLE? HOW FAR BACK?_____

_____

6. WHY DO I REFUSE TO GIVE THIS LOVE?

_____

7. THE GRACES I NEED TO HANDLE NO. 3, 4, 6 ABOVE ARE

   3. _____

   4. _____

   6. _____

8. HOW HAVE I RESPONDED TO THESE GRACES GIVEN IN THE PAST? _____

_____

9. I HAVE ASKED GOD'S FORGIVENESS AND THE FORGIVENESS OF THOSE I HAVE

HURT. I ASK THE CHURCH TO PRAY FOR ME. _____

10. I WILL DO THE FOLLOWING TO INTENSIFY MY STRUGGLE TO LOVE

_____

_____

1. AS I NOW SEE IT, GOD IS CALLING ME TO BE MORE LOVING AND RESPONSIVE

BY _____

_____ _____

2. WHOSE RIGHT TO TRUST AND LOVE DID I VIOLATE?

_____

INDIVIDUAL/GROUP

3. WHAT DID THIS PERSON HAVE A RIGHT TO EXPECT FROM ME AS A LOVER?

_____

4. HOW HAVE I FAILED TO LOVE ENOUGH SINCE MY LAST CONFESSION? (BE SPE-

CIFIC) _____

_____

_____

_____

_____

5. IS THIS PART OF A LONGER STRUGGLE? HOW FAR BACK?_____

_____

6. WHY DO I REFUSE TO GIVE THIS LOVE?

_____

7. THE GRACES I NEED TO HANDLE NO. 3, 4, 6 ABOVE ARE

    3. _____

    4. _____

    6. _____

8. HOW HAVE I RESPONDED TO THESE GRACES GIVEN IN THE PAST? _____

_____

9. I HAVE ASKED GOD'S FORGIVENESS AND THE FORGIVENESS OF THOSE I HAVE

HURT. I ASK THE CHURCH TO PRAY FOR ME. _____

10. I WILL DO THE FOLLOWING TO INTENSIFY MY STRUGGLE TO LOVE

_____

_____

1. AS I NOW SEE IT, GOD IS CALLING ME TO BE MORE LOVING AND RESPONSIVE

BY _____

_____

2. WHOSE RIGHT TO TRUST AND LOVE DID I VIOLATE?

_____

INDIVIDUAL/GROUP

3. WHAT DID THIS PERSON HAVE A RIGHT TO EXPECT FROM ME AS A LOVER?

_____

4. HOW HAVE I FAILED TO LOVE ENOUGH SINCE MY LAST CONFESSION? (BE SPE-

CIFIC) _____

_____

_____

_____

_____

5. IS THIS PART OF A LONGER STRUGGLE? HOW FAR BACK?_____

_____

6. WHY DO I REFUSE TO GIVE THIS LOVE?

_____

7. THE GRACES I NEED TO HANDLE NO. 3, 4, 6 ABOVE ARE

    3. _____

    4. _____

    6. _____

8. HOW HAVE I RESPONDED TO THESE GRACES GIVEN IN THE PAST? _____

_____

9. I HAVE ASKED GOD'S FORGIVENESS AND THE FORGIVENESS OF THOSE I HAVE

HURT. I ASK THE CHURCH TO PRAY FOR ME. _____

10. I WILL DO THE FOLLOWING TO INTENSIFY MY STRUGGLE TO LOVE

_____

_____

1. AS I NOW SEE IT, GOD IS CALLING ME TO BE MORE LOVING AND RESPONSIVE

BY _____

_____

2. WHOSE RIGHT TO TRUST AND LOVE DID I VIOLATE?

_____

INDIVIDUAL/GROUP

3. WHAT DID THIS PERSON HAVE A RIGHT TO EXPECT FROM ME AS A LOVER?

_____

4. HOW HAVE I FAILED TO LOVE ENOUGH SINCE MY LAST CONFESSION? (BE SPE-

CIFIC) _____

_____

_____

_____

_____

5. IS THIS PART OF A LONGER STRUGGLE? HOW FAR BACK? _____

_____   _____

6. WHY DO I REFUSE TO GIVE THIS LOVE?

_____

7. THE GRACES I NEED TO HANDLE NO. 3, 4, 6 ABOVE ARE

3. _____

4. _____

6. _____

8. HOW HAVE I RESPONDED TO THESE GRACES GIVEN IN THE PAST? _____

_____

9. I HAVE ASKED GOD'S FORGIVENESS AND THE FORGIVENESS OF THOSE I HAVE

HURT. I ASK THE CHURCH TO PRAY FOR ME. _____

10. I WILL DO THE FOLLOWING TO INTENSIFY MY STRUGGLE TO LOVE

_____

_____

1. AS I NOW SEE IT, GOD IS CALLING ME TO BE MORE LOVING AND RESPONSIVE

BY _____

_____

2. WHOSE RIGHT TO TRUST AND LOVE DID I VIOLATE?

_____

INDIVIDUAL/GROUP

3. WHAT DID THIS PERSON HAVE A RIGHT TO EXPECT FROM ME AS A LOVER?

_____

4. HOW HAVE I FAILED TO LOVE ENOUGH SINCE MY LAST CONFESSION? (BE SPE-

CIFIC) _____

_____

_____

_____

_____

5. IS THIS PART OF A LONGER STRUGGLE? HOW FAR BACK?_____

_____

6. WHY DO I REFUSE TO GIVE THIS LOVE?

_____

7. THE GRACES I NEED TO HANDLE NO. 3, 4, 6 ABOVE ARE

    3. _____

    4. _____

    6. _____

8. HOW HAVE I RESPONDED TO THESE GRACES GIVEN IN THE PAST? _____

_____

9. I HAVE ASKED GOD'S FORGIVENESS AND THE FORGIVENESS OF THOSE I HAVE

HURT. I ASK THE CHURCH TO PRAY FOR ME. _____

10. I WILL DO THE FOLLOWING TO INTENSIFY MY STRUGGLE TO LOVE

_____

_____